--3

Colin --

Such a pleasure serving with you --

Thanks for all you do for our church --

Steve --

Acknowledgments and Thanks

Many thanks to my God and my family for support and love beyond measure.

For Sara, my dear wife,
whom I love and fight for.

And to my children and grandchildren.

Self Defense Scenarios

Staying Alive in a Dangerous World

Skip Coryell

Published by White Feather Press. (www.whitefeatherpress.com)

ISBN 978-1-61808-212-1
Cover design created by Ron Bell of AdVision Design Group (www.advisiondesigngroup.com)

White Feather Press

Reaffirming Faith in God, Family, and Country!

Books by Skip Coryell

We Hold These Truths
Bond of Unseen Blood
Church and State
Blood in the Streets
Laughter and Tears
RKBA: Defending the Right to Keep and Bear Arms
Stalking Natalie
The God Virus
The Shadow Militia
The Saracen Tide
The Blind Man's Rage
Civilian Combat - The Concealed Carry Book
Jackpine Strong
Concealed Carry for Christians
The Covid Chronicles: Surviving the Upgrade
The Covid Chronicles: Surviving the Apocalypse
The Covid Chronicles: Surviving the Solstice
The Mad American - Judgment Day
The Mad American - Day of Reckoning
Sunrise Reflections: Finding Hope in Hard Times
Self Defense Scenarios: Staying Alive in a Dangerous World

Contents

1. Home Invasion..1
2. Parking Lots..15
3. Child Abduction.....................................29
4. My Daily Walk..43
5. ATM Robbery..57
6. Dog Attack...71
7. Road Rage...85
8. Multiple Assailants..................................99
9. Civilian Combat.....................................115
10. Concealed Carry for Christians..........123

From the author

Summer, 2022

The world has always been a dangerous place but ... doesn't it seem like it's getting more and more dangerous by the day? It certainly seems that way to me.

I've been teaching concealed carry classes for over 20 years, with over 18,000 students under my belt, and the number one reason people take my class, according to them, is this: "It's just getting too scary out there, and I feel I can't put off getting a gun any longer."

Fear motivates. Fear of death motivates even more.

But fear of death, fear of being beaten; fear of being raped; they're not the only fears my students face. There's also a secondary fear, and they talk about it in my classes all the time. "What happens if I make the wrong call? What happens if I'm attacked and I don't know what to do?"

Those are excellent questions.

Here's what I've learned. In the moment of

truth, when the violent criminal jumps out from behind the dumpster, shoving a gun into your face, you won't have perfect, cognitive thought. You won't be able to make a calm, rational decision on what to do. That's why we train and study well before disaster strikes.

It's vitally important that all of us know what to do prior to the self-defense event. Every day we should study the crimes that are most likely to be enacted on us. We need to study the criminal mindset. Famous, Chinese philosopher Sun Tzu tells us the importance of knowing our enemy. But he also tells us we must know ourselves.

We are all different in many ways. What works for me might not work for you. So you have to figure out, in advance, what works for you in any given self-defense scenario. And that's what this book is all about.

Evil exists. Some day evil will visit you. What will you do when that happens? Your actions on that day will determine whether you live or die ... whether or not the ones you love will survive.

In every chapter of this book, I use my novel-writing skills to vividly create a self-defense scenario, to paint a story so clear and compelling that it entertains you. In the Tactical Analysis, I use my 20-plus years of self-defense training and experience to break it down for you and answer the questions:

1. What did the person do right?
2. What did they do wrong?
3. What should I do in a similar situation?

There's also a special page at the end of each chapter where you can record your own thoughts and ideas on what you should do if you're ever in that scenario.

Most concealed carriers don't study or practice; they simply blunder into a life-changing event, believing the mere presence of the gun will save them. They believe that when evil visits they'll rise to the challenge to a level above their training.

Please don't make that mistake. Study and train hard so that when evil visits your door, you'll know exactly what to do and how to do it. That is my hope for all who read this book. Train hard – train often.

God bless and stay safe.

– Skip Coryell

Jonathan backed away from the door and walked over to his gun safe. His hands were shaking nervously, so it took him three tries to get the combination right. Finally, he opened up the safe and pulled out his Taurus Judge revolver.

1. Home Invasion

JONATHAN HAD LIVED ALONE his entire adult life, never marrying, never forming lifelong bonds. But that didn't mean he was unhappy. To the contrary. He had his job at the neighborhood grocery story, which he liked very much. He worked in produce, and enjoyed stocking the displays and keeping the fruits and vegetables fresh. He'd already retired from his manufacturing job of 30 years, and was drawing his pension, social security and 401k. The job at the grocery store gave him a little extra cash, but also got him out of the house and gave him a reason to get up in the morning.

It was 2AM on a Friday night when Jonathan heard the pounding on his front door. He'd stayed up late watching a documentary on the American Revolution, so when he heard the pounding and the yelling on his front porch, he didn't immediately jump up and run to investigate. Like many people in their mid-60s, Jonathan sat up slowly in bed, and struggled to bring himself into the waking world. He'd learned from experience to wake up slowly and gradually, knowing that if he tried to jump up out of bed in a hurry, the sudden change in blood pressure could make him feel dizzy. His back hurt, so he reached around to rub it before swinging his legs over and letting them drop down onto the floor.

The screaming was louder now, so he walked quickly downstairs to the front door. He peeked through the small window of the front door and saw a man he didn't know. The man was yelling through the door as he pounded on it with his fists.

"Let me in, Sandy! I need to talk! I can't live without ya, baby!"

Jonathan shook his head back and forth as he stepped away from the door. He thought about it for a second, deciding what was best to be done. He considered calling the police, but he knew if he did that, they'd take 20 minutes to get there, then they'd interview him and he might even have to appear in court. He didn't want the hassle of all that. He decided to talk to the man through the door.

"Hey buddy. You got the wrong house. Sandy isn't here."

The man responded by kicking the door with

his boot. “What the hell are ya doin’ in there with my girlfriend? Let me in or I’ll break down the door!”

Jonathan responded. “Stop kicking the door, man. Yer gonna break it. Just go away before I call the police.”

But that response seemed to set something off inside the man and he screamed and kicked even harder.

Jonathan backed away from the door and walked over to his gun safe. His hands were shaking nervously, so it took him three tries to get the combination right. Finally, he opened up the safe and pulled out his Taurus Judge revolver. It felt heavy in his hand, and it seemed to give him confidence. That’s when he noticed the man was no longer yelling or kicking the door.

Jonathan moved back to his front door and peeked outside, but he saw no one. He contemplated going back to bed, but he wanted to make sure the man was really gone. He unlocked the front door and stepped out onto the porch, holding the pistol in front of him. He looked nervously first to the left and then the right, but saw no one. For a few more seconds he listened, then turned to step back inside. That’s when the man screamed and leaped out of the bushes. He knocked Jonathan down onto the concrete porch and began punching him in the face over and over again while screaming.

“I’ll kill ya, man. I’ll kill ya!”

Jonathan tried to cover his face with his left hand but his attacker was younger and stronger. Finally, in desperation, he lifted the gun to the man's stomach and began pressing the trigger on his Taurus Judge. He pressed five times, and the roar deafened him so much he didn't hear the clicking of empty cylinders until the man's body collapsed down on top of him. Blood flowed all over him as Jonathan struggled to get off from under the corpse.

Finally, he managed to squirm out and bring himself up to his knees. He looked down at the man he'd shot, his lifeless eyes staring vacantly up at him. Bile rose up into his throat as he turned his head to the bushes and began to vomit uncontrollably.

Taurus Judge

The Taurus Judge is a 5-shot revolver chambered in .45 Long Colt and .410 shotgun shells. Hitting the market in 2006, Taurus International (headquartered in Brazil) promotes The Judge as an anti-carjacking gun and also an excellent tool for home defense. It weighs 29 ounces unloaded with a barrel length of 3 inches and overall length of 7.5 inches. Normally the BATFE would classify The Judge as a short-barreled shotgun, thus making it illegal, but The Judge has a rifled barrel which makes it exempt from that classification. Despite that, The Judge is illegal under California state law.

Since 2005, Taurus has developed several other models of the gun including a smaller version called The Public Defender, as well as the Raging Judge which is chambered for .454 Casull, .45 long Colt and 3" .410 shot shells.

Because of its weight and size, The Judge is not usually carried in a holster, but is more likely to be found at home in a gun safe or in the glove box or console of a vehicle.

The stainless steel version of The Judge has a manufacturers suggested retail price of $615.37.

Answer the questions:

What did Jonathan do right?

What did he do wrong?

TACTICAL ANALYSIS

THERE ARE A LOT OF THINGS JONATHAN DID right and a few things he can improve on. Let's start with the praise first.

<u>What did Jonathan do right?</u>

1. **He gave himself time to wake up before entering into the fray.** This may sound trivial, but it's important, especially for many of his age, because he needed to be at his best. He needed to be sharp mentally so that he could make the best possible decisions while entering into combat. He also needed to wake up his body as well. As you age, your body doesn't perform as well as it used to in many regards. Think of it like this. I have two pickup trucks. One is brand new and runs like a top. When I press the accelerator it responds with as much speed as I want. My other truck is 20 years old. It's my beater and I use it for hauling wood. When I start it in the morning it has to turn over a few times before starting up, and then I have to let it warm up a few minutes before driving away. Most 65-year-old bodies are like that. They were great back in the day, but they just don't perform cold as well as they used to. How do I know this, well, because I'm 65 years old.

2. **He peeked through a small window to see who was at the door.** This too sounds trivial, but it's not. Before you go into battle you should first count the cost. In the military we call that gathering intelligence. If you have incorrect intel, then you're likely to lose the battle. He was wise to discreetly peer out onto the front porch before making his presence known. For all you know he could be pointing a high-powered rifle at the door just waiting for you to speak. Or, there could be several attackers instead of just one.

3. Most importantly, he didn't open the door to a stranger. Instead, **he spoke to the man through the closed and locked door.** While doing this, move to one side, putting the frame of the door across your spine and vital organs. Most handgun rounds will penetrate your front door, but not the double two-by-fours of the door frame. In the self-defense world we call this type of conversation *verbal judo*. It allows you to gather more intel about the person's frame of mind and his intentions. If you do it properly, it can also put him on the defensive.

4. **He told the man he was calling the police.** This puts the attacker on notice and in many cases will prompt them to flee. A better way to say it would've been like this" I've already called the police and they're on their

way. They'll be here any second." Now he has to make a decision that directly affects his present and his future.

5. When the situation began to escalate, when the verbal judo failed, **Jonathan moved to the gun safe and retrieved his firearm**. It probably took him about 5 seconds to do this and that's time well spent. The actual fight took only 3 to 5 seconds, and once that started there was no opportunity to go to the gun safe.

6. After Jonathan opened the door and stepped outside, he looked around but didn't see the attacker. Then he was jumped from behind and in a sudden wrestling match with the attacker. Once he realized he was no physical match for the attacker, **he used his firearm to prevail**. He knew beforehand that it was legal for him to shoot in this scenario, and he also knew that he was willing to shoot at a moral level. If you decide ahead of time what is legal and what is moral, then you won't hesitate when the moment of truth comes. You'll do what you need to survive. But if you haven't thought about it in advance, then you spend precious seconds trying to make these decisions under stress. It's best to figure these things out prior to the heat and confusion of combat. Jonathan had done his homework.

What could Jonathan improve?

There's really only one big thing that Jonathan did wrong: he left the safety of his home and gave away two big advantages.

1. **Physical Protection. Jonathan left the safety of his castle**, unlocked the door and walked outside. This put him on an even playing field with the home invader. If Jonathan had remained inside his home, then the criminal would've been forced to either flee or kick down the door before gaining entrance. Jonathan would've been better served by putting himself behind cover (something that would stop a bullet and hide him) and then letting the man come to him. When police respond to a crime scene and find signs of forcible entry, it bolsters the claims of the home owner when he says he was forced to shoot.

2. **Legal Protection**. When Jonathan walked out of his home, **he also forfeited the legal protection offered by something called Castle Doctrine**. Most states have a statute pertaining to Castle Doctrine, and it lowers the thresh hold for use of deadly force in your own home. But the moment Jonathan walked out the door, that extra layer of protection was gone.

Castle Doctrine

[kas-uhl dok-trin]

Noun

A legal doctrine that allows a person to use deadly force in protecting his/her home and inhabitants from an attack by someone intending to inflict serious bodily harm.

–legaldictionary.net

Summary - Jonathan did a great job right up until he walked out the door. That was a potentially fatal mistake on his part. If he'd stayed inside and called the police, they would've gotten there in time to handle it, or, the criminal would've fled, or, he would've broken down the door and entered just in time to be shot. All three possibilities are superior to the final outcome in this scenario.

Final score: 80% (out of 100)

Final Thoughts
What would you do?

Key Points to Remember

1. When faced with a deadly threat, stay inside your home for the added protection of Castle Doctrine.
2. Decide now when you are willing to use deadly force.
3. Set up your home like a castle with concentric rings of security moving outward.
4. Never open your door to a stranger.
5. Arm yourself first and then call 911.

Donald resisted as best he could, but the men had him outnumbered and were younger and stronger than him. The man at his door swung his hammer several times glancing blows off Donald's head and shoulders.

2. Parking Lots

DONALD WORKED FOR A large chain of Midwestern convenience stores. As such, he was the District Manager and traveled almost every day, doing much of his computer work inside his car in parking lots and sitting at uncomfortable restaurant tables. He enjoyed his job and the people he worked with, but not the constant travel. He'd seen lots of bad things go down while sitting in his car at gas stations and convenience stores, and that's why he'd taken a concealed carry class, gotten his permit and then bought a gun.

His everyday carry gun was a Glock Model 44. It was compact and light with a 10-round magazine chambered in .22 caliber long rifle. He carried it on his strong side in an inside the waistband holster. He practiced about twice a year but only fired a few rounds, just to make sure he could still hit the paper plate at 20 feet.

It was a Friday afternoon and he was on the road about 120 miles from home, getting ready to head back to his family. He'd just performed an annual evaluation on a store manager and it hadn't gone well, so he was grumpy and in need of some comfort food and caffeine. Donald parked his car and walked inside the gas station. Five minutes later he came out with coffee and donuts and sat in his car eating while he filled out the evaluation on his computer.

Normally, he tried to watch what was going on around him and to keep a heightened state of awareness, but this time he was so involved in his work that he didn't see the two men walk up behind his car until they were already there. When he finally did see them, he immediately, hit the doorlock button and felt a sense of relief as the locks engaged.

He made eye contact with the man at the driver's side door and a wave of fear came over him when he saw the rage and hatred coming from the man's eyes. He didn't see the man on the passenger side until he shattered the window, sending glass inside the car. Donald instinctively raised his hands up to shield his eyes, but it was too late. His face was already cut and bleeding, and he was momentarily blinded in one eye. He tried to wipe the blood away so he could see better, but it only made it worse.

The man closest to him shattered the window

with his own hammer, and now both men were reaching in trying to pull him out of the car. Donald resisted as best he could, but the men had him outnumbered and were younger and stronger than him. The man at his door swung his hammer several times glancing blows off Donald's head and shoulders. Donald heard the bone in his left cheek break and felt intense pain as he struggled. The man on the passenger side began hitting him as well. Donald moved to the middle and avoided the blows as best he could.

Finally, he remembered the pistol on his strong side and reached down to draw it, but fumbled with it. Overwhelmed by pain, it took him several seconds to get the gun out of the holster. Donald was then hit on the head squarely and almost lost consciousness. That gave the man on the passenger side opportunity to get a firm hold around Donald's throat and he was able to drag him out the window.

In one last desperate attempt, Donald pointed his Glock 44 behind him, firing blindly at his attacker. He fired 10 times into the man's abdomen and thighs until the man finally let go. The other attacker ran away and jumped into a waiting car which quickly sped off, leaving their colleague behind.

Donald reached up and wiped the blood away from his eyes so he could see better. He turned around and saw the man sitting on the pavement with the hammer still in his hand.

The Glock was at slidelock, and that made him feel incredibly vulnerable, even though the man wasn't getting up. Feeling very weak and in great pain, Donald backed away slowly and then staggered as best he could into the gas station for help.

Glock Model 44

The Glock Model 44 weighs only 16 ounces fully loaded, but has the look and feel of the bigger Glocks. It's a joy to carry and easy to shoot with hardly any recoil. It comes standard with 10-round magazines, but you can buy an aftermarket 18-round magazine as well.

The gun has a 4-inch barrel and a 6-inch sight radius, making it a fairly accurate gun. It has a hybrid steel-polymer slide which reduces weight.

I own two Model 44s, and my kids love to practice with them. They are quickly becoming a favorite of women who wish to carry concealed but don't want the weight and recoil of the larger Glock 19.

On the downside, .22 long rifle lacks the kinetic energy and stopping power of the larger calibers. We'll talk more about that in the tactical analysis.

Answer the questions:
What did Donald do right?

What did he do wrong?

Tactical Analysis

There are a lot of things Donald did right and a few things he can improve on. Let's start with the praise first.

What did Donald do right?

1. **He tried as much as possible to maintain a heightened state of awareness.** Unfortunately, it's impossible to always be on full alert, especially when working on a computer or a cell phone. We'll discuss later things he could have done to enhance his awareness.

2. **He took the trouble to train, buy a gun and get his concealed pistol license.** We'll talk later about his choice of gun and whether or not it was right for him.

3. **He locked his door** as soon as he sensed possible danger.

4. **He had his gun readily accessible** on his strong side in a good holster.

5. **He moved to the center of the car** to make it more difficult for his attackers to strike him with the hammers.

6. **He had no moral qualms about shooting the attacker**, because he'd thought it out

in advance.

7. He drew his gun and **he took the only shot he had**, and he fired until the threat stopped.

8. As soon as he could safely do so, **Donald retreated to safety** by entering the gas station for help.

<u>What could Donald improve?</u>

Donald did well enough to survive the attack, but he could have done much better and possibly avoided injury or the altercation altogether. Here are some changes he could easily make to enhance his security.

1. **Avoid parking lots.** Parking lots are a transitional space. A transitional space is defined as any area where you move from one relative area of safety to another. This could be your driveway, a parking garage, ATMs or even walking down the sidewalk. Parking lots are one of the places where criminals sit in their car, watching people come and go in order to pick out their next victim. Donald made a habit of working in parking lots, and that put him at unnecessary risk. He would've been better served to work at a cafe or a restaurant in clear view of the public.

That being said, there are times when you have to sit in your car. When that happens, here are some things you can do to mitigate the risk.

- Adjust your side-view mirrors and rear-view mirrors so you can see everything behind you, and check your mirrors often.
- Park in full view of other people and don't let your car get blocked in.
- Park in full view of security cameras. This can act as a deterrent to thieves.
- Buy several motion sensor alarms. You can get a set of 4 for under 30 dollars. Put them on your car front and back as an early warning system to allow you to focus on your work.

2. Practice more shooting and practice drawing from the holster. Practice shooting every week. Practice should include sighted fire, unsighted fire, shooting from unorthodox positions, one-handed shooting, as well as moving to cover and shooting from behind barricades.

Caution: Get formal training from an expert before doing this on your own.

When the moment of truth came, Donald couldn't draw his gun under stress. You need to practice drawing your pistol thousands of times and make it muscle memory. That way when you get nervous, you do it automatically without thinking.

3. Choose a gun with more firepower. Some people are forced to shoot .22 caliber pistols for many reasons (weak hands, recoil sensitivity, arthritis, carpal tunnel, etc.) but Donald is not one of those people. Most pistol instructors recommend that you carry the highest caliber that you can safely and accurately control. Most people can carry a .380 or 9mm with no problem. Donald could've done that as well. He chose the .22 caliber because he was lazy and didn't want to be bothered with the larger and heavier pistol. At the very least he could've bought an 18-round magazine and had rounds left for the second attacker. As it was, he got lucky when the second man chose to flee instead of attacking him with the hammer.

4. Improve your diet and exercise. Donald's lifestyle, always on the road and always eating fast food, is not conducive to open-handed fighting. A healthy, fit person is harder to kill, but Donald was out of shape and quickly tired during a physical fight for his life.

5. Get some open-handed skills. Donald didn't have the skills to physically fight against two men. Some type of martial arts training would've served him well in this fight. Some good ones are Mixed Martial Arts, boxing, wrestling, Jui Jitzu and Krav Maga. All of these are good in confined spaces and rely more on gross motor skills instead of fine motor skills.

Summary - Donald did a good enough job to save his life, but he never should have put himself in that situation in the first place. Avoid transitional spaces like the plague. Donald got lucky and he survived, but it wasn't because of his superior skills and training. Job #1 for Donald is to get more training: combat pistol and open-handed skills. He also needs to buy a gun that is better suited for him. At the very least, have a gun with more firepower inside his car where he can quickly access it.

Final score: 73% (out of 100)

Final Thoughts
What would you do?

Key Points to Remember

1. Don't spend a lot of time in transitional spaces.
2. Carry a gun with adequate firepower, as much as you can control and be proficient with.
3. Maintain a heightened state of awareness.
4. Get some open-handed skills. You may have to fight your way to your gun.
5. Get in shape and stay in shape.

About halfway through the shopping excursion, Sandra got a creepy feeling, like she was being watched. She looked up and over to her left and saw a man looking at her.

3. Child Abduction

When Sandra had first found out she was pregnant, she'd been disappointed. Not because she didn't want kids, but because she just had so many other plans that would now have to be put on hold. But what happened next surprised her. The moment her little girl was born and she held the tine bundle in her arms, she'd immediately fallen head over heels in love with her little girl.

She took her 2 months of family leave, and the bond between her and her daughter continued to grow. Finally, when it was time for her to return to work, she'd shocked her husband by quitting her job and announcing she was now a stay-at-home mom. Her husband was even more surprised when she bought a gun and took a concealed carry class in order to get her permit to carry. When he asked her why she was doing this, she simply answered, "This is my daughter and she's depending on me to protect her."

Her daughter, Anna, was now 8 months old, and Sandra had the perfect life: a great husband, the cutest daughter in the world, and a lifestyle that allowed her to enjoy herself and her family. Her new career was to take care of her family, and she loved it.

That morning, Sandra took Anna to the grocery store for their weekly shopping trip. She put Anna in the cart, and pushed the cart through the store as she piled items inside, always getting the best price, always reading the ingredients to make sure her family got the best nutrition.

About halfway through the shopping excursion, Sandra got a creepy feeling, like she was being watched. She looked up and over to her left and saw a man looking at her. Initially, she smiled, and he smiled back. But his look lingered too long, and it made her feel uneasy. Finally, the man turned away and walked out of sight.

Sandra shook it off and went back to her job of buying groceries for her family and playing with her little girl. She was relieved when she didn't see the man again, and by time she reached the checkout counter, she'd totally forgotten about him.

A few minutes later, she reached their minivan and buckled Anna into her car seat. She left the side door open so her baby could feel the breeze as she loaded the groceries into the back. Sandra was halfway through loading the groceries into the back hatch when she heard the sound of a van door sliding open. She took a step to the right and looked on as the same man she'd seen inside the store stepped out of the van beside her own van and started to unbuckle her daughter from her car seat. She hadn't noticed people inside because the van had tinted windows.

Sandra's first feeling was terror, and that lasted about 2 seconds. Then, when she saw her little girl in the arms of a stranger, her terror turned suddenly into anger.

She yelled as loud as she could. "Hey. Stop!"

But the man didn't stop. He jumped quickly into the back seat of the van and the electric door slid shut as the engine fired up. Sandra could hear her daughter crying inside the stranger's van.

Quickly, she drew her Smith and Wesson Model 642 revolver from her fanny pack. The van was backing up now, and Sandra could see the woman driver as she turned the steering wheel and moved the shifter from reverse into drive. Knowing she had only a split second to save her daughter, Sandra fired a single round into the front, passenger-side tire, making it go immediately flat. Sandra ran to the driver's side door, and aimed her pistol through the window at the driver and yelled for her to stop.

Inside, she heard her baby crying. Then the man yelled out to the driver. "Just go! Run over the b$tch!"

The female accomplice put both her hands

back on the steering wheel, and Sandra didn't hesitate. She pointed the gun at the woman's chest and fired one round into the driver, hitting her center mass. The driver's side window shattered, sending glass everywhere. Sandra saw the blood on the woman's chest right before her head slumped forward into the steering wheel. The van rolled slowly forward and crashed into her own mini-van.

Other shoppers were gathering closer now, so Sandra yelled as loud as she could. "They stole my baby! They got my little girl!"

An older man she didn't know stepped forward as he drew his own pistol and aimed it at the van.

"Don't shoot into the van. My baby is in there!" The man nodded his head and pulled on the door handle. Both Sandra and the good samaritan aimed their guns into the van, and when the door was fully open, they saw the kidnapper scrambling to open the door on the other side. They held their fire. Her baby was on the floor crying. Sandra holstered her gun and ran forward and scooped up her child.

The kidnapper escaped but was later picked up by police. Her baby was unharmed.

Smith & Wesson Model 642

The Model 642 is a classic self-defense gun. It's chambered in .38 special and has plenty of kinetic energy to make close-range center-mass shots. It's not designed for long range, but with practice, most people can easily hit a paper plate at 20 feet, so long as they have good eyesight and don't have a problem handling high recoil.

Five-shot revolvers are designed as an anti-mugging device. They are very good at taking out one attacker at close range. Here are the gun's pros and cons:

Pros:

- The .38 special round hits very hard.
- Small and light and easy to carry
- Inherently safe, reliable and dependable
- Easy to shoot

Cons:

- Low ammo capacity
- Heavy recoil
- Heavy trigger press
- Not accurate at longer ranges

Answer the questions:

What did Sandra do right?

What did she do wrong?

Tactical Analysis

There are a lot of things Sandra did right, but there is always room for improvement, so let's break it down and learn from her terrible experience.

What did Sandra do right?

1. **She was legally armed.** In this scenario, if Sandra hadn't been armed her daughter would've been abducted and never seen her mother again. She needed the gun to save her daughter.

2. **She had fairly good situational awareness**. When she was unloading her groceries, she heard a sound and investigated. If she hadn't done that, she might have never known what was happening and the kidnappers would've succeeded in stealing her daughter.

3. **Sandra channeled her anger into something useful**. Instead of falling apart emotionally, Sandra had a strong protector-defender mindset. She unleashed the warrior inside her and that helped her focus on what needed to be done to save her daughter.

4. **She had very little hesitation.** Sandra had thought this out in advance. She knew her reason for being armed was to protect her

daughter, so when she saw the threat, she immediately went to guns. She had practiced in advance, so her drawstroke was smooth and proficient.

5. **She shot the front tire.** This was a much better idea than shooting the driver or the kidnapper who was holding her daughter. The van had tinted windows, so she would've been firing blinding and maybe killing her daughter instead of saving her. Even if they'd gotten away, the criminals wouldn't have gone far with a flat, front tire, thereby making it easier for the police to rescue her daughter.

6. As soon as the driver was in view and it became obvious she wasn't going to stop the getaway car, Sandra ran to get in the proper position to shoot. She knew her daughter was in the back seat, out of the line of fire. **Sandra followed the safety rule, "Always know your target and what is beyond."**

7. **Sandra had no moral dilemma.** She'd obviously thought this out ahead of time, and knew that she was willing to use deadly force to save her daughter. Many people never take the time to ask them self, "When am I willing to use deadly force?" Instead, they wait until the threat happens and they hesitate. Sometimes making a moral decision of that magnitude can take months or even years,

and you won't be able to do it under extreme duress and in a split second. Sandra didn't hesitate. She fired.

8. Sandra had good verbal skills. Throughout the encounter, Sandra spoke with firmness and clarity and with strength. She yelled for the man to stop. When a crowd started to gather, she yelled "They stole my baby! They got my little girl!" Many times the crime scene is confusing and bystanders don't know if you're the good guy or the criminal. Sandra removed all doubt when yelling this. When the good samaritan drew his gun, she took tactical control, "Don't shoot into the van. My baby is in there!"

9. She let the kidnapper go. Every fiber of my being wanted her to shoot the kidnapper, but she did the right thing in restraining herself. One criminal was down and the other was fleeing. Because of the extreme circumstances, she may have gotten away legally with shooting the second kidnapper, but perhaps not. It all depends on the jurisdiction and the laws of your state. Aside from that, she didn't have a good shot and panic fire sometimes hits innocent bystanders.

What could Sandra improve?

Sandra was awesome, but there are a few things she could have done to make her performance even better..

1. **Always trust your gut instincts.** Inside the store she saw the kidnapper, and she felt uneasy about the interaction. When someone seems creepy or scary to you, then listen to that inner voice and go on high alert. The times in my life where I've ignored my gut instincts are also the times when I've made major mistakes and gotten into trouble. She could've asked the store manager or one of the employees to walk her out to the car. Most stores will accommodate you in a situation like that.

2. **She left the sliding door open.** When she left the door open, her daughter was in plain view. In this case the crime was pre-planned, but many crimes are crimes of opportunity, so don't give criminals an extra opportunity to hurt you or your family. Close and lock your doors whenever possible.

3. **Never park beside vehicles with tinted windows:** It's possible that the van parked beside her after she'd gone into the store. Regardless, go out of your way to leave an open space on either side of your vehicle. When someone parks beside you, there's only about 3 or 4 feet of space between you

and the car beside you. That hems you in and cuts off your escape route.

Summary - Sandra did an incredible job saving her daughter. The amount of stress she was feeling must have been tremendous so the fact that she performed as well as she did is amazing and she is to be commended. You're never going to perform flawlessly under stress, but Sandra came pretty close.

Final score: 96% (out of 100)

Final Thoughts
What would you do?

Key Points to Remember

1. Don't dawdle in transitional spaces. Get in and out quickly.

2. Carry a gun and get as much training and practice as you can. Also, practice shooting under stress.

3. Always trust your gut instincts, and when you feel uncertain, maintain a heightened state of awareness.

4. Get professional training shooting in and around vehicles.

5. Decide when you are willing to use deadly force and when you are not.

6. Know the laws of deadly force in your state.

The man reached behind her, grabbing her by the hair and started to drag her back into the woods, but she raised up the pepper spray and let loose with a steady stream until the can was empty.

4. My Daily Walk

SAMANTHA WORKED AT A big advertising firm in town, and sometimes it was stressful with very firm and unforgiving deadlines. Because of that, everyday she just had to get away from her desk for a while to relax and get her head in the right spot again so she could do a better job.

So every day at exactly 10;15AM she took a walk through the park a few blocks from work. Samantha was meticulous and a creature of habit. She loved her routine, and it gave her comfort, knowing that she'd get that break. On the way to the park there was small cafe, so she'd stop and buy a honey oat milk latte, and then she'd add just a dash of cinnamon ... not too much, not too little, but just the right amount. And then she'd sip it while walking to the park.

Samantha was big on personal security, and she'd gone to a women's self-defense seminar on how to make your life safer. As she approached the park, she shifted her latte to her left hand and reached down into her small purse and adjusted her key ring and her pepper spray for easy access. And then she walked down the trail to the right, through a small copse of trees, past the playground to a more secluded portion of the park where she could be alone and think.

As she approached her destination, she was relieved to see that no one was sitting on her park bench. Every once in a while another person was there, and it aggravated her to no end. But it was empty today, so she walked over and sat down on the uncomfortable wooden bench. Samantha set the timer on her cell phone for 7 minutes, then she sipped her latte, closed her eyes and just felt the slight breeze on her face. It blew a lock of her hair down across her eyes, but she didn't fix it. As she sat thinking about anything except work, the stress and tension began to melt away.

Seven minutes later, her timer went off, and she reluctantly pressed the button to turn it off. She took another sip of her drink, then looked around one last time before getting up and walking back the way she'd come.

As Samantha entered the copse of woods, a movement off to her right caught her attention. It was her experience that sometimes children wandered off the trail and played in the woods, so she thought little of it. Then she saw the movement again, and this time it was much closer.

Something inside her made her feel uneasy, uncomfortable, but she still saw nothing of certainty to alarm her.

Regardless, she reached down into her purse and put the pepper spray into her right hand. There was a trash can up ahead, so she dropped the half-empty latte cup into it as she walked by. Suddenly, a man exited the woods about 20 feet in front of her, and came running toward her. Samantha was startled, not knowing what to do. She raised up the pepper spray with her right hand, but she held off on deployment, simply because she was surprised and didn't know what was happening. The man looked like a jogger, but why was he in the woods?

When the man crashed into her she was knocked violently to the ground onto her back. The man reached behind her, grabbing her by the hair and started to drag her back into the woods, but she raised up the pepper spray and let loose with a steady stream until the can was empty. The spray was ineffective at stopping the attack, and once inside the woods the man let go of her and quickly straddled her, effectively pinning her to the leaf-covered woods floor.

That's when Samantha finally heard herself screaming. She must have been screaming all along, but for some reason she just didn't hear it. The attacker then raised up his fist and began beating her about the face and chest until she went silent. He warned her that if she screamed again he would kill her.

The pepper spray had little effect on the man, because his back was turned as he drug her into the woods. That's when Samantha noticed the tears streaming down her face and the burning on her cheeks. Some of the spray had been blown back toward her and she could hardly see the man on top of her.

At that point, Samantha gave up the fight and complied with whatever the man demanded in the hope that he would let her live if she cooperated.

Two days later, some children playing in the woods found her body. The police never identified the attacker.

Pepper Spray

Pepper spray is the most popular less-than-lethal self-defense tool on the market. It's especially popular with women. While it's an effective tool in certain scenarios, it was never meant to be a replacement for a gun. Most altercations don't rise to the level of deadly force, and in those scenarios pepper spray is a very nice thing to have in your hand. For example, a man gets in your face and starts screaming at you and making physical threats. At that point you can't just shoot him, but you can pepper spray him.

Pepper spray is effective on roughly 80 to 90 percent of the general population. But it will be less effective on hardened criminals who've built up a tolerance to it or have a high pain threshold and can fight through it. It will also be less effective on people under the influence of drugs and alcohol.

Here are my recommendations:

1. Buy the strongest pepper spray allowed in your jurisdiction.

2. Buy a large cannister, not the tiny one that goes on your key ring.

3. Make sure the safety device is quick and easy to deploy with one hand while under stress.

4, Aim for the eyes and nose.

5. Use a pepper gel which is less effected by the wind and rain.

6. Remember that pepper spray rarely shoots as far as advertised.

Answer the questions:
What did Samantha do right?

What did she do wrong?

Tactical Analysis

There are a few things Samantha did right, but she made some mistakes that resulted in her death. Let's start with the good.

What did Samantha do right?

1. **She had some training.** Samantha went to a women's seminar on self-defense. They likely taught her about situational awareness, pepper spray and how to gouge someone with their car keys. That's a good start, but doesn't go far enough.

2. **She had fairly good situational awareness**. Samantha was fairly alert as she moved through the park, and it was obvious that she took her personal defense seriously. When she saw the movement in the woods, she went on high alert and tried to figure out what was going on.

3. **She trusted her gut feeling**. When she felt threatened, she put her pepper spray in her right hand and got it ready for deployment. This probably saved her 2 or 3 seconds once she recognized the threat.

What could Samantha improve?

.

1. **Choose more than one self-defense tool.** Samantha's choice of pepper spray as her only tool was ill-advised. Pepper spray will protect you in a non-lethal attack, but this attack was anything but that. In this scenario, Samantha desperately needed a gun or a knife. Since it was hands-on, close quarters combat, either would have done the job, although a gun is easier to use for most women as you need only 6 pounds of trigger pressure to deploy it. Some people over-estimate the effectiveness of capsaicinoid sprays, and it proves to be their downfall. My experience has been that many women rely solely on pepper spray because they are afraid of the gun or have some political bias against it. It's always good to have more than one self-defense tool on your person. Ideally you want a knife, a gun, pepper spray, some open-handed skills, a confident warrior mindset and a heightened situational awareness. Samantha needed a self-defense system instead of just one tool.

2. **She went alone.** Just ask yourself one question: How many women is a serial rapist looking for? The answer is simple - just one. Two women is one victim and one witness. I know she wanted to be alone to unwind and

to collect her thoughts, but we can't always safely have what we want. Even if a girlfriend had been along, it would have acted as a deterrent. Rapists don't want to get caught, so they avoid groups and prefer the lone woman. Always travel in a group whenever possible.

3. She chose a secluded area to walk. Serial rapists don't like to be bothered while they're raping women for obvious reasons. Even though Samantha screamed as loud as she could, there was no one to hear her. Sometimes screams sound innocent, like kids playing or adults laughing or even a wild animal. And let's face it, most people are hesitant to be good Samaritans these days. It's not unusual for people to avoid getting involved when someone is being attacked. Sometimes people will come to watch and perhaps even videotape your attack and then put it on social media. You can no longer count on the protection of others as good Samaritans are becoming fewer and farther in between.

4. She allowed herself to be patterned. This is one of the worst things a person can do. Never set up a lifestyle that is totally predictable to a stranger. I've been an avid deer hunter for most of my life, and I understand that any deer can be killed, if it can be patterned. Before I can harvest that deer,

I need to know where it's going to be at a certain time of the day. In order to achieve that, I do something called pre-season scouting. I sit up in a treestand and watch the food plots: the corn or hay or soybean fields and I take notes. When I see a big buck walk into the field, then I note the time and location.

This is the same thing serial killers and serial rapists do. They sit in the parking lot and watch who goes in and out, taking notes and watching for patterns.

Most of us are creatures of habit. It makes us feel secure, like we're in control of our lives if we can set up a schedule and live it out. Ironically, the thing that makes us feel secure, in reality, puts our lives in more danger.

Anyone can be killed. If they can be patterned; they can be killed. Samantha should have mixed up her schedule. She should've gone to different places in the park and always varied the time. But because she was always at the same place at the same time, the killer knew exactly how to ambush her.

Summary - While Samantha did have some good things she was doing, in the final analysis, she died. She had some good awareness and a good instinct, but she didn't possess the proper tools nor the proper training to survive this scenario. Some mistakes are survivable, are more forgiving, but allowing yourself to be patterned by a serial killer and then going into his domain alone without the proper skills and tools is something that few people can live through.

Final score: 58% (out of 100)

Final Thoughts
What would you do?

Key Points to Remember

1. Don't rely solely on pepper spray to save your life. Create a system of self-defense that is tailor-made for you and your lifestyle.
2. Carry a gun and get as much training and practice as you can. Also, practice shooting under stress.
3. Always trust your gut instincts, and when you feel uncertain, maintain a heightened state of awareness and retreat to a safe place.
4. Avoid being patterned. Mix up your schedule.
5. Avoid secluded areas and don't travel alone unless you have no choice.

The stranger closed the distance and reached his right hand out from behind his back and brandished the knife in front of him. It was about a foot long with a 6-inch double-edged blade.

5. ATM Robbery

IT WAS 10 O'CLOCK AT NIGHT and Paul was meeting some of his college friends for a few drinks at one of their favorite restaurants downtown just a few blocks from the campus. On the way there he realized he didn't have any cash on him, and he needed to pay back his friend the 20 dollars that he'd borrowed from him last week. So on the way there, he stopped at an Automated Teller Machine (ATM). It was one of those machines just outside the bank on the edge of the sidewalk.

Paul's father had taught him to always be aware of his surroundings, and he usually was pretty good at seeing trouble before it visited him. But today Paul's mind was distracted. He had all kinds of problems. He wasn't getting along well with his girlfriend and he suspected that she was about to break up with him. On top of that, he'd just gotten a poor grade on one of his finals and his scholarship was now in jeopardy.

As he walked up to the ATM, Paul remembered to be alert and he looked behind him and then all around. He'd been taught that going to ATMs, especially late at night was a risk, so he put his personal problems aside and renewed a heightened sense of awareness. Seeing no one around, he walked up to the machine and took out his wallet. He took his book pack off and set it on the concrete beside him. He inserted the ATM card and waited for the prompts.

Just then, he heard a car pull up on the road behind him. Paul knew this was a no-parking zone, so it struck him as odd that a car would pull up and stop. Quickly, he glanced over his shoulder and saw a car stop right in front of the ATM. As he watched, a man in his late twenties or early thirties got out of the car and walked toward the machine. At first, Paul thought the man just wanted to use the ATM, but the man didn't politely stop and wait at a distance behind him as was customary. He kept coming. And then Paul saw the look on the man's face, and immediately he was filled with fear. The man's face was stern, almost angry, and then the man smiled and stopped just an arm's reach away from Paul. That's when he noticed that the stranger's right hand was hidden behind his back.

Paul had a gut feeling that something bad was about to happen, so he backed up a step. He stopped backing up when he bumped into the cement block wall of the bank. The stranger closed the distance and reached his right hand out from behind his back and brandished the knife in front of him. It was about a foot long with a 6-inch double-edged blade.

Immediately upon seeing the knife, Paul sprinted to his left as fast as he could. The man reacted quickly, as if he'd been anticipating this and stabbed Paul in the arm. The blade cut through Paul's jacket and into the muscle of his right bicep, but Paul kept running as fast as he could.

He could feel the blood flowing down his arm, but that didn't stop him. Paul had been running track all through high school and still held the school record for the 400-meter dash.

As he neared the end of the block, he glanced over his shoulder and saw the attacker standing at the ATM machine pushing buttons. Paul noticed that his breathing was labored and that his heart was racing much faster than it should have for just a short sprint. At this point, Paul stopped and watched as the man withdrew Paul's daily limit of cash. A part of Paul wanted to run back and try to stop him, but the blood flowing down his arm and onto the sidewalk made him think twice.

He needed medical attention and he'd survived. All he had to do was keep running away. And then a thought came to him. Paul hid behind the corner of the building and then reached into his back pocket and pulled out his cell phone. He quickly took a 5-second video of the man as well as the getaway car and the license plate.

Then he called the police as he jogged toward the cafe up ahead on the left. He walked inside and yelled for help. Several of the diners looked up at him but did nothing. Then a woman rushed up to him and took control. She identified herself as an emergency room nurse. She asked him what happened, then did an assessment before rendering first aid. She stopped the bleeding and Paul was rushed to the hospital.

Types of Knives

dirk

[durk]noun

a dagger, especially of the Scottish Highlands.

dictionary.com

stiletto

[sti-let-oh]noun

plural sti·let·tos, sti·let·toes.

a short dagger with a blade that is thick in proportion to its width.

dictionary.com

dagger

[dag-er] noun

a short, swordlike weapon with a pointed blade and a handle, used for stabbing.

dictionary.com

switchblade

[swich-bleyd] noun

a pocketknife, the blade of which is held by a spring and can be released suddenly, as by pressing a button.

dictionary.com

Butterfly knife

A type of folding pocketknife that originated in the Philippines. Its distinct features are two handles counter-rotating around the tang such that, when closed, the blade is concealed.

wikipedia.com

Answer the questions:

What did Paul do right?

What did he do wrong?

Tactical Analysis

All things considered, Paul did a pretty good job handling this scenario. Nonetheless, there is room for improvement. Let's start with the good.

What did Paul do right?

1. **He had pretty good situational awareness.** Paul was distracted by personal problems on the walk to the ATM, but upon arrival, he pushed the manual override button in his brain and forced himself to look around and check for threats. No one can be at a heightened state of awareness at all times, but in high-risk scenarios, we have to force ourselves to be alert.

2. **Paul trusted his gut instincts**. When he heard the car pull up behind him in a no-parking zone, an alarm went off in his head, and he turned around to look. If he hadn't done this, he could have been stabbed from behind without any warning. Because he turned around, he had an extra 5 seconds to prepare himself emotionally for what was about to happen. Time gives you options.

3. **Paul ran away**. This was undoubtedly

Paul's best tactical option, because it played to his strengths. He was a track star and, because he was in his early twenties, still in shape and in his prime. He had no open-handed skills, so he couldn't fight back or defend in that way. He had no other defensive weapons like a gun or pepper spray or a knife. His only other choice was to comply and trust in the good graces of the man who was brandishing a knife and robbing him. Choosing to run is probably what saved his life. Even martial arts practitioners hesitate to try to disarm violent attackers with a knife, as it takes a great amount of skill to do so, and many times it results in getting cut.

4. **Paul videotaped the attacker**. Once he'd created sufficient distance, Paul hid behind the corner and recorded the attacker in the process of a crime. He also had the presence of mind to include the car and the license plate number. The wound on his arm was a concern, but it was a muscle cut and no major arteries were severed, so he did have 30 seconds to spare, Because he did this, now the police have a chance at catching the criminals, and putting them behind bars so they can't victimize more citizens.

5. **Paul suppressed his ego**. There are certain things not conducive to making rational self-defense choices. Drugs, alcohol and

ego. Every morning I take my pistol out of the gunsafe and place it in my holster. Then I reach into my chest and rip out my ego. I place it in the gunsafe and I leave it there all day long. Your ego will prod you into making bad decisions that could result in your death. Don't listen to it. Even after Paul had fled to safety, his ego tempted him to return into a dangerous situation while the attacker was stealing his money. He overrode his ego, and he survived because of it.

6. **He fled to the cafe**. After making a successful escape, Paul retreated to a populated environment where he could get medical help. At this point he really didn't know how badly he was injured, so it was paramount that he get treated medically. Fortunately, the cafe had an ER nurse who could stop the bleeding and make him stable before transport to a hospital.

What could Paul improve?

1. **Paul had no self-defense tools.** Paul's only tools in this scenario were his speed and his situational awareness. It turned out to be sufficient against a knife, but what would have happened if the attacker had been brandishing a gun instead of a knife? He could have shot Paul as he ran away. One lucky shot and Paul is dead. I don't think we can

fault Paul too much in this scenario, because he's a college student and most colleges are pistol-free zones. This is just one more situation where pistol-free zones get innocent people hurt and protect violent criminals.

2. Paul lingered in a dangerous space. ATMs and parking lots are two of the most dangerous places you and I can frequent. They are called transitional spaces, and that's where criminals go to stake out their next victim. They'll sit in a car nearby and watch until they see someone they feel is an easy target. The number one rule when out and about in public is this: If you look like sheep, you'll be eaten by wolves. Aside from that, avoid parking lots and ATMs. Think about it. An ATM is tailor-made for an armed robber. They want your money. You are at an unprotected portion of the bank withdrawing it for their convenience. Most of us can't go about our day-to-day lives without using a parking space, but if we plan ahead, we can avoid ATMs.

3. He let the attacker get too close. Paul knew something bad was about to happen, but he froze up while the attacker was closing the distance. If this happens to you, it's okay to create space and use your voice as a warning. I understand that he didn't want to leave his ATM card unattended, but in this case it would've saved him a stab wound to the arm. In a loud and firm voice yell for them to: "Stop," or "That's far enough." or "Please wait until I'm done." Do this while holding up your hand in front of you with your palm up for emphasis. An innocent person just there to use the ATM will comply, but a criminal will not. If they keep advancing, then you have a more concrete idea of his intentions.

4. **Paul didn't call 911**. I know it's a lot to ask, especially when you've been robbed, stabbed and had a near-death experience, but he could have punched in 911 and given the police a head start on their investigation while he was moving to the cafe.

Summary - All things considered, Paul did a great job. He survived a deadly attack by using his situational awareness, and by thinking clearly and soundly. No one is going to be perfect in this scenario, but all things considered, Paul did well by using his strengths to escape and living to fight another day.

Final score: 87% (out of 100)

Final Thoughts
What would you do?

Key Points to Remember

1. Avoid ATMs at all costs. They are just too dangerous and not worth the risk.

2. Situational awareness is key to survival. Don't be caught off guard, especially in transitional spaces.

3. Always trust your gut instincts, and obey them. If your gut says retreat, then do so.

4. If you can legally carry a self-defense tool, then make it happen, and carry every day.

5. It's sometimes best to retreat and avoid the altercation altogether.

6. Never underestimate a knife. They are as deadly as guns.

7. Don't trust your ego. It will write checks that your body can't cash.

Carol tried to jerk her hand away, but the dog's jaws were too powerful, and it began to back away, bending her lower to the ground. Carol screamed as loud as she could in hopes that someone would help, but no one came.

6. Dog Attack

Carol was in her late twenties and she had it all: a good job at a local bank, a husband that adored her, a nice house in the suburbs, and she was 2 months pregnant with their first child. Carol had run cross country and track all through high school and college, and she still liked to walk or run every day just to unwind and to stay in shape.

It was 7AM on Saturday, and she wanted to take a long jog before starting the day, so she donned her sweatsuit, kissed her husband on the cheek as he still slept and headed down the block for a 5-mile run.

She lived in a sleepy neighborhood, some would say boring, but there was very little crime here. In fact, in the 2 years they'd lived here, she couldn't recall hearing about any crime in their neighborhood at all. Carol felt safe here, and she liked not having to worry about being victimized by bad people.

Carol was about halfway through her run now, so she turned around at the midway point and started heading back. There was a large, colonial house up ahead on the right that she always admired on her run, and she secretly harbored hopes of being able to afford a house like it some time in the future.

As she approached the house, she was surprised to see a large dog on the sidewalk blocking her path. It hadn't been there just a few seconds ago. She chopped her step and slowed to a walk. The dog was about the size of a German Shepherd but it had a large head and neck and broad shoulders. It was facing her, and its short ears were propped up as it stared at her.

Though Carol had never owned a dog, she also had never had a bad experience with a dog. But this dog was very large and she couldn't help but be extremely nervous about his presence. She looked around for the owner, but saw no one. Carol stopped to give herself some time to think. In the end, she decided that discretion was the better part of valor, and she turned to the left and walked out onto the road to go around the dog. The dog trotted out to meet her, and Carol stopped in her tracks. She remembered someone from the past telling her to never show fear to a dog, that they could smell it. But she didn't know what to do, because she really was afraid.

The dog was standing in front of her now, cutting off her path. She looked into the dog's eyes but that gave her no clue as to what she should do. She remembered that dogs were very focused on the sense of smell, so she reached her right hand out, palm down, to let the dog sniff the back of her hand. The dog growled softly.

Carol's hand stopped in mid-air. She decided to talk softly to the dog, trying to reassure him that she meant him no harm. The dog backed up a step and hunched its back. Carol took another look around for the owner, but saw no one. She extended her hand out a bit further, but the dog growled again.

Fear rushed through Carol's mind as her heart rate began to escalate. She decided to try and walk around the dog and put him behind her. With her hands dropped down to her side, she stepped to the left a few feet and walked around the dog. The dog followed her. Carol stopped and the dog began sniffing her legs.

In another attempt to assuage the dog's fear Carol reached her hand out to pet him. Immediately and without warning, the dog bit into her hand and held on. Carol tried to jerk her hand away, but the dog's jaws were too powerful, and it began to back away, bending her lower to the ground. Carol screamed as loud as she could in hopes that someone would help, but no one came.

Carol was on the pavement now and the dog was growling and thrashing his head from side to side. Blood was everywhere, on the road, the dog and all over Carol. She kept screaming as loud as she could, but still no one came. Carol had pepper spray in her right pocket but couldn't get to it with her left hand.

It was at that moment that Carol realized this could very well be a life-or-death situation. She began punching the dog's head with her left hand, but it was her weak hand and it had very little effect on the dog. By now the dog had drug her up to the curb and was still pulling, all the while growling and shaking its head from side to side.

Carol was on her stomach now, facing the pavement. Just to her left she noticed a rock about the size of baseball. She scooped it up with her left hand and began hitting the dog's head over an over again with it, but the dog's grip remained firm.

Finally, the rock made contact with the dog's eye and he immediately let go and ran off. Carol lay on the pavement for several seconds, trying to catch her breath and calm down. Then she noticed the blood pooling around her hand. That's when a car pulled up and stopped. A man got out of the car to help Carol while his wife called 911.

Dog Attack Statistics

Here are the top 5 breeds with the most bite attacks in the United States.

1. Pit Bull - These dogs are the most abused breed in the US, because some are born and bred to be used in the illegal dog fighting industry. 65% of all dog-bite fatalities come from Pitbulls.

2. Rottweiler - These are typically good-natured dogs, but if not socialized and exercised properly, they can become aggressive.

3. German Shepherds - German Shepherds are high energy, alert, with protective instincts, but if not properly trained are more likely to bite humans they don't know.

4. Presa Canario - Used as guard dogs and in illegal dog fighting, they have aggressive instincts.

5. Wolf-dog Hybrids - They are less domesticated than canines, and half wild, making them more aggressive. They are more likely to attack when scared or defensive.

Dogs most often in bite statistics possess these physical characteristics:

- Strong musculature
- Muscular cheeks
- A large, strong jaw
- A wide mouth
- A large head
- Strong hindquarters

Answer the questions:

What did Carol do right?

What did she do wrong?

Tactical Analysis

Carol did some good things, but she also made some mistakes that escalated the dog attack. Let's look at the good first.

<u>What did Carol do right?</u>

1. **She made a good effort to stay in shape.** Many people after college let their bodies get out of shape. Carol exercised regularly and that can go a long way in self-defense. A healthy, fit person is harder to kill. She had a strong cardiovascular system, plus more muscular strength than the average woman because of her efforts.

2. **She had fairly good situational awareness**. She noticed things going on around her. She was naturally curious and took note of the houses and the environment. Because of this, she noticed the dog right away and didn't blindly blunder into it.

3. **She carried a less-than-lethal weapon**. Every time I go out into public, I carry my pepper spray on my left side. I do this be-

cause my gun is on the right, and I may have to quickly transition to guns during the fight. Carol didn't have a gun, so she carried on her strong side. Unfortunately, she was unable to bring the pepper spray into the fray because her right hand was in the dog's mouth.

4. **She tried to go around the dog**. This was a good tactic. In general, you should always try to avoid altercations, whether they are human or animal. She made a good attempt to avoid the dog, then tried to walk away, but the dog followed. Sometimes avoidance and escape don't work, and that's where your weapons come in.

5. **Carol didn't give up the fight**. Once the fight started, Carol fought with ferocity. She punched the dog as hard as she could repeatedly. Unfortunately, her left arm was too weak for the job. It's a good idea to build up the strength in your weak side as well as your strong side.

6. **Carol screamed**. Not only did she scream, but she screamed as loud as she could and she didn't stop screaming for help until the threat was over. Many times no one comes to your aid, but sometimes they do. Think about it this way: If you don't ask for help, then the answer is always no.

7. **Carol used improvised weapons**. She

had the presence of mind to see the rock and to understand that the rock was a weapon she could use to save her life. A rock used against a human or a dog can cause death or serious bodily injury. Always look around you and be aware of weapons in your environment that you can use to save your life.

What could Carol improve?

.

1. **Choose more than one self-defense tool.** Just like Samantha in the previous story, Carol's choice of pepper spray as her only tool was ill-advised. Pepper spray can protect you in a dog attack because a dog's olfactory senses are very keen and their noses are highly sensitive. Spray them in the nose, and many times a dog will leave. Just understand that it's not always effective, and carry a back-up tool like a pistol or a knife (preferably both) just in case the less-than-lethal method fails. When I jog or walk, or even while walking through a parking area, the pepper spray is always in my hand and ready to deploy. If Carol had done this one thing, then she may not have been bitten at all. As soon as she saw the dog, then pepper spray should have come out of her pocket and into her hand. Just like a gun, if you can't get to the pepper spray in time, then

it's like you don't have it. All your self-defense tools should be readily accessible.

2. **Carol offered the dog her hand.** She extended her hand out to a dog that she didn't know. This is rarely wise. You have no idea what the dog's history is or what it's capable of. To compound the problem, she offered the dog an open hand. She should have kept her hand in a fist, making it harder for the dog to grab onto the hand. An open hand in a dog's mouth is easy to hold on to and will result in more tissue damage, blood loss and nerve damage. It's quite possible that Carol will need several surgeries to repair the damage to her hand.

3. **Carol didn't heed the dog's warning.** When a dog growls, it's trying to talk to you. It's telling you that he doesn't feel comfortable or that he's afraid, and that whatever you're doing, you should stop. When a dog is nervous, they growl. If they're protecting something, they growl. This was an obvious pre-attack indicator that Carol should've followed, but because she had so little experience with dogs, she had no idea what to do. All of us would be well advised to become proficient in the canine language. Most dogs aren't wild animals that want to bite you. Learn to read their body language.

4. She stopped walking away. Carol did the right thing when she tried to go around the dog. It would've been even better if she'd backed up slowly and gone home another route. Never turn your back on an aggressive dog, and never hold eye contact with a dog. In the animal world this is often seen as a challenge. Also don't smile widely at the dog. Humans see this as non-threatening, but dogs see it as a pre-attack indicator. Why? Because dogs keep their mouths dropped open when they're relaxed, but when they are aggressive, their mouths spread wide and lips tighten and they bare their teeth. To a strange dog, your friendly smile looks like a dangerous snarl.

Final score: 81% (out of 100)

Final Thoughts
What would you do?

Key Points to Remember

1. Don't rely solely on pepper spray to save your life. Create a system of self-defense that is tailor-made for you and your lifestyle.

2. Carry a gun and get as much training and practice as you can. Also, consider carrying a knife as a back-up tool.

3. Stay alert and avoid altercations. Go around the dog or retreat when possible. Don't turn your back on the dog and don't run. It will trigger the prey/predator instinct and he'll chase you.

4. Once the fight starts, never give up. Unleash your own inner beast and fight with all you have.

5. Learn to look for and use improvised weapons. Anything heavy and blunt or sharp can be used as a weapon.

6. Take 15 minutes to research and understand dog language. It could save life or limb.

Tom, now totally out of control and feeding off his own rage, reached in with both hands and tried to pull the man out of the cab of the pick-up truck.

7. Road Rage

TOM WAS 34 YEARS OLD AND AL-ready a partner at his law firm in Dallas. His wife was one of the top real estate agents in the Dallas-Fort Worth metropolitan area. They had two kids in private school, one in 2nd grade and the other in kindergarten.

As he glanced down at the clock in his Mercedes S-580, he knew he was in trouble with his wife again. He was supposed to pick the kids up from the after-school care and he was running 15 minutes late. He thought to himself, *If I can just get out of this traffic, then I can make up some time on the freeway.*

He glanced quickly into his rear-view mirror before pressing the accelerator. The driver behind him honked his horn, but he quickly left him far behind. Tom had always loved the feel of power that his car gave him, and his wife told him that his personality changed when he got behind the wheel. He didn't think so though. He was the same guy no matter what he was doing. Tom had always been competitive in everything he did whether he was playing tennis or driving or trying to win for his clients in court. It was just part of who he was.

All was going well until he saw the accident up ahead. It was just a little fender bender, but it had everything backed up for a quarter mile at the traffic light. He slammed both palms against the steering wheel in exasperation.

Quickly, he glanced around, trying to find a way around the traffic jam, but he couldn't see any alternate route. Tom was growing more and more frustrated and angry by the second. He tried in vain to calm himself down, but then he looked at the clock again. He was now 20 minutes late.

After 2 more minutes of waiting, he decided to get creative. He backed up just enough to give him room, and then he cut the steering wheel to the right and hopped up onto the shoulder of the road. He just had to drive the quarter mile up to the stop light then he could get around the accident and be on his way to pick up his kids.

Tom's Mercedes was up to 45 miles an hour, and he was just a hundred yards from the stop light when one of the vehicles in line suddenly pulled onto the shoulder and blocked his path. Tom slammed on his brakes and barely kept from hitting the pick-up truck, stopping just a few feet from the truck's back bumper. It was an older truck with dents and rust all around the bumper and rear quarter panels. The pick-up truck moved forward again and Tom followed closely behind him.

Tom's rage grew to full bloom when he saw the man raise his middle finger and hold it there in defiance. Tom wanted to ram him from behind, but knew his Mercedes would suffer the lion's share of damage if he did. Instead, he just honked his horn angrily and raised his own middle finger while staying just a few feet off the man's back bumper.

Just then, the driver of the truck slammed on his brakes. Tom was unable to stop in time, and the front of his car crashed into the old pick-up truck. Parts of the grill flew out and away and the hood crumpled upward like an accordion. And that's when Tom lost any semblance of self-control.

The truck ahead didn't move, so Tom opened his door and ran as quickly as he could up to the driver's window and started screaming profanities at the other driver. The man just laughed at Tom and that infuriated him even more. Then the man flipped him off again, and Tom pulled back his right fist and punched the man's window. It shattered glass into the man's eyes and he bowed his head closer to the steering wheel, blood dripping from his face.

Tom, now totally out of control and feeding off his own rage, reached in with both hands and tried to pull the man out of the cab of the pick-up truck. Other drivers were exiting their vehicles now and some were already recording it on their cell phones. One man walked over and yelled at Tom to stop, but Tom couldn't hear him. There was an intense pressure on his ears that wasn't normally there.

The man was pulled halfway out the window now, but was holding on to the steering wheel with both hands, so Tom pulled as hard as he could and finally managed to get the man out onto the pavement. Tom straddled the other driver and began pounding his already bloody face with his fists. Tom was so focused on his rage, that he didn't hear the 70-year-old bystander yelling at him to stop.

All of a sudden, Tom heard a loud pop, and then experienced a feeling of being punched in his left shoulder. He paused from beating the other driver and saw blood on his left bicep. And then he felt it again, this time in his left side. He looked up and saw the old man holding a pistol. Tom's anger immediately subsided and was replaced by fear.

Tom stopped beating the man and rolled himself off and onto the pavement. He could hear the sirens now as he waited on his back. The old man was staring down at him, still pointing the pistol at his face. He looked over at the other driver and noticed for the first time that he'd been punching an old man.

A sinking feeling ran through the pit of his stomach, as he realized he might be a lot later than he'd first anticipated.

Aggressive Driving

Aggressive driving is a factor in 54% of all fatal motor vehicle crashes, according to the AAA Foundation for Traffic Safety

78% of drivers report committing at least one aggressive driving behavior in the past year. (AAA)

The most common types of road rage are tailgating, yelling or honking at another vehicle, and are a factor in more than half of all fatal crashes.(AAA)

In a seven-year period, road rage incidents caused 218 murders and 12,610 injuries. (AAA)

Running late is one of the leading reasons given for aggressive driving.(NHTSA)

There are an average of about 30 road rage deaths per year.(AAA)

Road rage is on the rise, with a 500% increase in fatalities resulting from aggressive driving crashes between 2006 and 2015.(NHTSA)

Men self-report more aggressive driving behaviors than women on average.(AAA)

Drivers under the age of 40 are most likely to commit road rage. (AAA)

Answer the questions:
What did Tom do right?

What did he do wrong?

Tactical Analysis

This scenario is a bit different than the others, because we really have two players here: Tom, the aggressive driver, and the old man in the pick-up truck. Neither of them did anything right, so we'll just skip over the positive.

<u>What did Tom do right?</u>

1. **Absolutely nothing.**

<u>What did Tom do wrong?</u>

1. **Tom lost control of his temper.** This man is a self-absorbed narcissist who is high on his own abilities and his own success. Many people have two personalities: their normal personality, and the one they drive with. There is something about getting behind the wheel of a powerful car that makes people feel stronger than they really are and unaccountable for their actions. The same thing happens when people are on social media. They say things they wouldn't normally

say, and they do things they wouldn't normally do. This combination of arrogance and lack of accountability is a recipe for disaster. Tom needs to understand that he is accountable for everything he does with his car and that he's not entitled to special rules or treatment. When you get mad at another driver, imagine they are bigger and stronger than you and holding a gun. If you do that, you may feel more accountable for your actions. And if that doesn't work, imagine the other driver has two dead bodies in his trunk, and he's looking for a place to bury them.

2. **Tom drove aggressively.** When Tom cut off that first person in traffic, you can argue that "Hey, that's how people drive in the big city during rush hour." And that's true to a point. But Tom didn't stop there. After that he pulled onto the shoulder of the road and started passing other cars. This made the other drivers angry, because they were waiting and he broke the rules to get ahead of them.

3. **Tom reacted to the pick-up driver after being flipped off.** Tom was being a jerk, but he still could've de-escalated the altercation by backing off. The pick-up cut him off, so Tom honked his horn and started to tail-gate him. Tom should've backed off and regained his cool. If he'd done that, then the truck driver would've went on his merry way

and Tom could've followed him around and out of the traffic.

4. Tom escalated the altercation. Every time one of these two players did something aggressive, the other would double down and take it to the next level. It usually takes two to tango, and this scenario was no exception. If either one of these men had backed off, then the harm could've been mitigated. Part of the problem here was ego. Every morning I go to my gun safe and pull out my pistol and holster it. Then I dig my right hand into my chest and rip out my ego. I place my ego inside the gun safe and I leave it there all day. Guns and ego don't mix and neither do cars and ego. When you get behind the wheel of your car, you need to become the most polite person on the planet

5. Tom was the first to become physical. Up until now, the altercation has been aggressive, out of control and just flat-out childish, but Tom anxiously took it to the next level. He took it from verbal insult to physical harm. There's a big difference between flipping someone off as opposed to punching their window and dragging them out of the vehicle. Tom crossed a line that can get you arrested and thrown in prison. It can also get you shot and sent to the hospital or maybe even killed. While threatening someone verbally is a crime (assault) carrying out that threat is a greater crime (battery). This was the point of no return for Tom; he'd just crossed the Rubicon so to speak.

6. **Tom didn't obey the armed bystander.** When you're in the process of beating up an old man, and a good samaritan points a gun at you and tells you to stop; stopping is a good idea. But herein lies Tom's Achilles heel. He was so consumed and driven by his own rage, that he couldn't hear the man commanding him to cease and desist. Tom was probably experiencing something called auditory exclusion. This occurs during times of great stress when you get a dump of adrenaline into your bloodstream, causing your heart rate to increase significantly. In addition to that, he was probably also suffering from tunnel vision. This is caused by the same escalated heart rate and extreme stress, causing Tom to lose his peripheral vision. All Tom could see was the man he was beating on the ground. So Tom didn't hear the challenge command and he didn't see the man pointing a gun at him.

Summary - Tom has a lot of problems that he needs to deal with. First and foremost his lack of self-control. Tom needs an anger management class, perhaps even psychiatric help. Now that

Tom is in the hospital and prison after that, he'll have an opportunity to get the help he needs. Over the next few years, Tom will have plenty of time and opportunity to analyze his performance and to make some positive changes in his life.

But Tom wasn't the only problem in this scenario. The old man who was beaten must also share in the blame. Neither of these men were heros or role models to be emulated. The pickup truck driver also drove aggressively when he went onto the shoulder of the road, then flipped off Tom and slammed on his brakes causing the crash. If the older, good samaritan hadn't shot Tom, the truck driver may have been killed for his part in the altercation.

\

One thing I always ask of my concealed carry students. Ask yourself this question: What is worth dying for? Most of us won't die to protect our ego and neither should you.

Tom's final score: 0% (out of 100)
Truck driver's final score: 20% (out of 100)

Final Thoughts
What would you do?

Key Points to Remember

1. Maintain self-control.
2. If you have trouble controlling your anger, then get professional help.
3. Don't drive aggressively. It makes other drivers angry.
4. If you feel yourself getting out of control, then do something to stop yourself.
5. Never react to an aggressive driver. Just let them go. It's not worth serious bodily injury, death or prison time..

The lead intruder was at his bedroom door now and already upon him. Connor pointed the pistol toward the man but didn't have time to get off a shot before being struck on the chest with the crowbar.

8. Multiple Assailants

Connor ran his own small business out of his house, because he liked the freedom of setting his own hours and the convenience of working out of his home. It also allowed him to spend more time with his wife and kids. Connor could've made more money working for a large corporation, but to him the money was less important than the time he spent with his family. Already at age 31, he'd been able to establish himself and make a modest living in his trade.

It was 11AM on a Monday, and Connor was working in his office in the basement of his home. He was getting good work done and feeling pretty good about it. His two kids were home schooled, but his wife had taken them to the library, so he was home alone.

Connor was just checking his email, when the dog started barking upstairs. Their dog, Murphy, was a 15-pound mixed breed, and Connor liked having the dog for the company, but also for the added security around the home. Connor looked up from his computer and hesitated. Murphy wasn't one of those small dogs that barked for no reason, so he got up from his office chair and headed upstairs to check it out.

He was expecting a package from UPS, so he moved to the front door and peaked out the small window. Much to his surprise, there were three men staring back at him. One held a crowbar, so Connor immediately backed away from the door. That's when one of the men slammed his body up against the front door. There was a loud crashing sound followed quickly by another. The door started to break away from the frame and Connor ran up the stairs to his bedroom.

Once upstairs, he went to his gun safe and punched in the six-digit code. The gun safe beeped and a red error light flashed. He could hear them coming up the stairs now, so he tried the combination again, this time with success. He opened the door and grabbed onto the Glock Model 17. The lead intruder was at his bedroom door now and already upon him. Connor pointed the pistol toward the man but didn't have time to get off a shot before being struck on the chest with the crowbar.

Connor felt his left collarbone give way as the bone splintered, but he fought his way through the pain, raised the gun up with his right hand

and pressed the trigger. All he heard was the resounding click of an empty chamber. That's when he remembered that his wife had insisted that he store it with an empty chamber for safety reasons. His wife had strong moral objections to guns, so Connor had offered to store the gun that way to make her feel less opposed to having a gun in the house.

The man raised the crowbar again and Connor turned his back to the attacker, allowing the crowbar to glance off his back. This time the sharp end of the steel cut into his rib cage, creating a large gash with lots of blood and also breaking one of Connor's ribs. Connor was able to rack the slide before being clubbed again, this time in the head. The second man was now inside the room by the doorway.

Connor raised his pistol up and fired three times into the man's torso. He dropped the crowbar and ran toward the bedroom door. The second man raised up a revolver and pointed it at Connor, and fired but his shot went wide to the left. Connor pointed with his gun hand and fired four times without aiming. The second attacker retreated out the door.

Jacked up on adrenaline and not thinking clearly, Connor fired three more rounds at the retreating man, even though he couldn't see him. He waited a few seconds to clear his thinking, then he got up and moved toward the bedroom door. Using the door frame as cover, he peeked around and looked down the stairs. At the bottom of the stairs, he saw a man crumpled up and bleeding.

Connor took stock of his injuries. He was bleeding from the head and chest, and the pain in his ribs and collarbone were almost unbearable. For a moment, he thought about going after the remaining two intruders, but thought better of it. He stepped back into his bedroom and leaned against the door frame for support. He did a quick assessment of his pistol to make sure that it was still operable. He wanted to call 911, but his phone was downstairs in the basement, and that would have to wait.

That's when he looked down the hall and saw the third man running toward him. Connor couldn't see if he was armed or not, so he retreated into the interior of the bedroom, firing three more wild shots. Once inside he put the bed between himself and the door. The intruder peeked into the bedroom. Connor raised his gun up. When the man saw this, he ran down the stairs as fast as he could. Connor shot three more times into the drywall out of fear.

He heard the door slam shut on the first floor, but he waited a full 5 minutes before leaving the room. On the way down he saw the dead man at the bottom of the stairs and another blood trail leaving his home. He staggered down to the basement and called 911.

Glock Model 17

The Glock Model 17 is a full-framed pistol. It's a bit bulky for everyday carry, but has some real advantages for home defense. The Glock 17 was the very first Glock. It was first introduced in 1982, and was controversial at the time, because it featured a polymer frame and was said to be undetectable by metal detectors. (This proved not to be true.) It was numbered 17 because it was Gaston Glock's 17th patent.

Here are the technical specifications:

- Caliber - 9mm
- Magazine capacity - 17
- Weight - 24.87 ounces empty, 32.28 loaded
- Barrel length - 4.49 inches
- Width - 1.26 inches
- Overall length - 8.03 inches
- Height - 5.47 inches
- Sight radius - 6.5 inches

Answer the questions:

What did Connor do right?

What did he do wrong?

Tactical Analysis

There are a lot of things Connor did right and a few things he did wrong. Let's start with the good.

What did Connor do right?

1. **He kept a dog for added security.** A good dog is an excellent supplement to your home security system, because a dog's keen senses can hear and smell things that you and I cannot. In this case, the dog was the first to alert Connor of the approaching danger. Without it, he would have still been inside the basement when the men broke in and would've been physically cut off from the master bedroom and his defensive firearm. A dog doesn't have to be large and ferocious to be an asset to home defense. They just have to serve as an early-warning system, and Murphy the mutt did just that.

2. **He didn't open the front door**. Connor didn't blindly open the front door, even though he was expecting a visit from the UPS

delivery man. Instead, he stood to the side and peered through the small window to see what was going on. One of the favorite tactics of home invaders is to simply knock on your front door and wait for you to open it before busting in and taking control. Never open your door to a stranger. Talk to them through the door until you are convinced they are safe to let in. If they don't go away, then call 911.

3. **He retreated to the safe room**. When it became obvious they were a physical threat, Connor retreated quickly to his safe room and tried to recover his firearm. He didn't think about it; he just did it. This means he'd already made a home defense plan in advance and simply had to follow it. Everyone should have a home defense plan, and make sure you share it with everyone in your home so they know what to do and when to do it.

4. **He had the right gun for the job**. The Glock Model 17 is a serious firearm, and it has been tested in battle for almost 40 years. One mistake people make in choosing a home defense gun, is they choose a low-capacity firearm, like a 5-shot revolver or a compact semi-auto. Your home defense gun can be big, bulky and heavy because you don't have to carry it concealed if you don't want to. It costs you nothing to let it sit in the gun safe ready to go. The Glock 17 is very

accurate with medium recoil and a 17-round magazine. Home invasions are more likely to involve multiple attackers, because they work in crews. Why? Because they are there to search your house and take everything valuable, and many hands make light work. There is also safety in numbers. In general, handguns are underpowered for personal protection, so it takes 3 hits to the upper chest to stop the threat. Connor had three invaders, so he needed 9 rounds, assuming he was a perfect shot under stress, which he was not. At the end of the gun fight, Connor had only one round remaining of his 17 rounds. Let's face it, no one ever comes out of gun fight saying, "I just wish I'd had less ammo."

5. Connor was mentally tough. He was brutally attacked by three men. He suffered a broken collar bone, a blow to the skull and a broken rib and lacerated back. Despite that, he was able to shake it off and keep fighting. Whenever you go into a fight, you should expect to get hurt, but giving up is not an option. Once you start fighting you are totally committed. You bite, you kick, you scratch you do whatever it takes to come out on top. Connor did an excellent job at this.

6. He shot well under stress. Connor shot well enough to come out on top. It's important to make your first shots count, and he did that. When the second invader saw his colleague bleeding in retreat, that slowed him down, causing him to think twice about what he was doing. Not all of Connor's shots were on target, but he killed one man and wounded a second. Most of the time you don't have to be perfect in a gunfight, but you do have to put good shots on target. Connor did that enough to survive. It was obvious that Connor had practiced.

7. He made good use of cover. Connor used cover well, and he understood the difference between cover and concealment. He knew that the door frames were made of double two-by-fours and that they would most likely stop a handgun round. Line up your spine with the cover, because everything vital is close to the center of your body. 85 percent of gun shot victims survive, but not those hit in the head, the spine or the heart.

8. He didn't pursue the armed felon. When the last invader fled, Connor was in no position to chase him down, because of his extensive wounds. His first instinct was to give chase, but this would have been foolish. In most cases, it's not a good idea to go after the armed felon. You've done your job. You survived. You protected your home and your family. Just call the police and let them take it from there. From this point on your job is to heal so you can defend another day.

What could Connor improve?

1. **Make the gun readily accessible.** Most people put their handgun in the master bedroom just like Connor, but you need to stage guns in locked safes throughout the house so you are never more than five seconds away from a loaded firearm. Also, opening the safe should be simple and fast. Under stress Connor entered the wrong combination. My gunsafes have either biometric technology or RFID (Radio Frequency Identification) technology. I just place my thumb on the sensor or wave the bracelet over it to open the gun safe. Hornady makes some excellent RFID gun safes in the 100 to 200 dollar price range. Get at least three and place them strategically around your home, at least one on every level.
2. **Store the gun ready to fire.** Connor's wife placed him in a precarious, even life-threatening situation by insisting that he store the gun with an empty chamber. I always tell my students that an unloaded gun is just a very expensive club. If you're in this situation with your spouse, do your best to work it out, because in the heat of battle, you probably won't have time to rack in a round before aiming and firing. The reality is this:

the gun is perfectly safe while sitting inside the gun safe whether the chamber is loaded or empty. During the gun fight, you're going to want the gun loaded.

3. He fired blindly at the retreating felon. Connor did this a few times and it was a mistake. Save your rounds for when you have the best chance of hitting the bad guy. Remember, when the gunfight ended, he had only one round remaining. In this scenario, Connor was the only family member home, but most times the rest of the family is there. In general, spraying bullets into the walls of your home can get your spouse and kids killed. Your shots should be aimed shots. I know that's tough under stress, especially when you're hurt and afraid for your life, but that's why we practice under stress with a competent professional. If you haven't yet taken some advanced classes where you have to draw, move and shoot and use cover, then by all means get it done.

Summary - Wow! This scenario was brutal and complicated, but Connor did a pretty good job, considering his injuries and all the stress he was under. It's not easy to shoot multiple assailants while you're bleeding and in a great deal of pain, but Connor did it well enough to kill one invader, wound another and drive off the third. He made a few mistakes, but his warrior mindset was enough to compensate, and he'd practiced sufficiently to put enough of the shots where they needed to be. Connor still has a way to go before he's the perfect protector-defender, but so do the rest of us. None of us are perfect, but if we survive and learn from our mistakes, then we can come back better and stronger next time.

Final score: 92% (out of 100)

Final Thoughts
What would you do?

Key Points to Remember

1. A high-capacity magazine for home defense is the better option.
2. Stage guns in locked safes around your house in strategic locations.
3. The gun must be loaded in magazine and chamber or it can't save your life.
4. Practice shooting under stress often so you can make well-aimed shots.
5. Understand use of cover and practice shooting from behind it.
6. Don't chase a fleeing felon. Call police and let them do it for you.
7. Never open your door to a stranger.
8. Dogs give you forewarning.
9. Mental toughness is as important as your gun. Never give up. You are the weapon.

Chapter 1

In this chapter you will learn the following:

- The definition of civilian combat and how it pertains to the concealed pistol carrier.
- The serious nature of civilian combat.
- The importance of situational awareness.
- The role of law enforcement in civilian combat.
- The extreme personal nature of deadly force training.

(Taken from dictionary.com)

civilian [si-vil-yuh n] – noun

1. a person who is not on active duty with a military, naval, police, or fire fighting organization.

combat [n. kom-bat] – noun

3. Military. active, armed fighting with enemy forces.

What is Civilian Combat?

WHY IS THIS BOOK TItled Civilian *Combat*? There are so many other things I could have called it … things less controversial, less prickly, easier on the ears. But … truth is, there's nothing warm and fuzzy about being shot with a gun or stabbed with a knife. The transition from civilian to combatant is huge, and very few people can do it with grace and ease. To the contrary, most people find it difficult, simply because they've been trained up and conditioned to believe that others will take care of them. Part of that stems from the urban culture we now live in, coupled with all modern amenities and technology we have at our disposal. We live in an instant society where everything we could possibly need or want is brought to us by simply pushing a few buttons. Need food? Pick up the iPhone and order some take-out. Want to watch the latest blockbuster movie? Order it on NetFlix.

But here's the problem. People have been conditioned to believe that law enforcement can and will protect them from all harm and wrongdoing. But the sad truth is they cannot. When you call nine-one-one, police officers are not instantly transported through your iPhone to your location where they handily and instantly dispatch the bad guys and save you and your family. Depending on where you are, the response time could be over thirty minutes. According to FBI crime statistics, the average fire fight lasts only three seconds, so if you're counting on the police to save you, you'll be sorely disappointed. While all good police officers want to help you survive in a deadly force situation, they cannot always be there, and they are not legally required to aid you. (Refer to the case "Warren Vs District of Columbia" for details.)

> Learning to protect your family is intimate and personal

The book is titled *Civilian Combat*, because

that's the best description of what you'll be forced to do when you're attacked. In all likelihood you'll be fighting alone against one or more attackers who are stronger, faster, younger and more aggressive than you. When I was a kid, I used to watch an old TV show in black and white called *The Lone Ranger*. At the end of the show, the good guy (Clayton Moore) always rode in on his white horse named Silver and rescued the damsel in distress or the down-trodden farmer who was being threatened by evil. The music they played during the preamble to the show and also during the rescue scene was the *William Tell Overture* and it just added to the excitement. But the truth of the matter is this: Evil exists, someday evil will visit your door. And when it does, the lone ranger will not be riding in on a white horse to save you, and you won't hear the *William Tell Overture* in the background. You are a civilian, but you are now locked in mortal combat. There is no cavalry. It's just you and whatever training, tools and mindset you brought along. You're on your own, because now, *you*, are the lone ranger. So, with that in mind, saddle up and let's get started.

When a civilian enters combat, he becomes a warrior.

> *"A fiery horse with the speed of light, a cloud of dust, and a hearty "Hi-yo, Silver, away!"*

Welcome to Class

AT THE BEGINNING OF EVERY CONCEALED carry class I teach, I go around the room and I ask each person three things: What is your name? What is your favorite thing to do? and Why are you taking this class? I don't do this because I'm nosy. I do it for two specific reasons:

1) IT HELPS THE STUDENT BOND TO THE INstructor. I've learned over the past fifteen years of teaching, that personal protection is, by definition, extremely personal. With well over 6,000 students under my belt, I've come to realize that it's natural for students to bond, in varying degrees, to the person who's teaching them how to protect their mates and their children from harm and death.

> The average fire fight lasts only 3 seconds.

It's not unusual for a total stranger to walk up to me and begin a conversation that goes something like this. "Oh, hey Skip! How's it going? It's been a long time. It's so good to see you again. What have you been up to?"

Almost always, this is a prior student of one of my concealed carry classes. I've become very good at nodding my head until I make the connection. But I always treat them as a friend, despite the fact I can't remember their name, because I know that on one special point in time we spent a day together on the range. And there's something incredibly bonding about shooting. I stood behind them, and to one side, as they began that most intimate of journeys, down the warrior's path, as they transitioned from sheep to sheepdog. Shooting firearms for personal protection is a growth experience, an American rite of passage, and, the very act of standing beside someone holding a deadly weapon … is the supreme act of faith and trust. I trust they won't shoot me, and they trust that I'll do my best to protect them against their own inexperience and that I'll teach them what they need to know to prevail in a life-or-death attack. Mutual trust and respect is the cornerstone of all the best relationships.

2) As a concealed carry instructor, at that moment in time, for that day, I am the most important person in their lives, and I need to be reminded of that. I'm not important because I'm good, I'm important because I'm teaching them to protect the people who are paramount in their own lives.

After teaching the same class for over fifteen years, the hundreds of repetitions can sometimes get to me. But I have to remember that even though I've said this same thing a thousand times before to others, this is the first and only time I'll say it to this particular group of individuals. And that, in itself, is special and personal, and can never be underestimated. I must always be at my best. I must always teach with the same fervor and excitement as I did when I first started teaching. Anything less is a disservice to my students. They trust me, and they depend on me to give them the best training available. And I always work to fulfill that realistic and necessary expectation. After all… this is life or death.

Things to Remember

1. The police cannot protect you at all times.
2. You are responsible for your own protection.
3. Civilians can and should be combatants.
4. Learning to protect yourself and your family is an intimate and bonding experience.

You can purchase “Civilian Combat: The Concealed Carry Book” on Amazon now. Available in paperback, hard cover, ebook and audiobook.

Joshua 1:9 (NIV)

Have I not commanded you? Be strong and courageous. Do not be afraid; do not be discouraged, for the Lord your God will be with you wherever you go."

Chapter 1
Courageous

WHEN I THINK ABOUT IT, really think about it, the one movie that has affected me in the most positive way is the 2011 movie by the Kendricks brothers called *Courageous.* I can still remember watching it for the first time, how I cried like a baby, how it silenced me before God and my family, how it moved me to change, to improve, to work harder and to take my responsibility as a father and a husband to a new level.

Now, sure, I'd always taken parenthood seriously, knew that being a dad and husband was one of the most important things I'd ever do, but ... the movie, the experience, is what inspired me to actually get out there and do my job better. There is something magical about the power of a good story. To the human soul, it inspires us, imbues us with power and courage and love.

And then there's that title song by the group *Casting Crowns*. The first line of that song is an incredible epiphany to me.

We were made to be
courageous.
We were made to lead the way.

What does that really mean? Here's how I break it down for myself.

1. We were made.

Psalm 139:14 (NIV)
I praise you because I am
fearfully and wonderfully made;
your works are wonderful, I
know that full well.

The Bible is clear throughout, from the very beginning, that we are not pond scum; we were not cosmic accidents; we didn't accidentally happen when a few enzymes and chemicals mixed together of their own accord and were zapped with electricity. We didn't just "happen." We were created, wonderfully made. And we were made by God, the most powerful force in the universe. Doesn't that knowledge change you? Encourage you? Humble you?

There is no stamp on your forehead that says "Made in China." The stamp is on our souls, and it says "Made by God ... in His image."

So God created mankind in his own image, in the image of God he created them; male and female he created them.

Genesis 1:27 (NIV)

2. We were made ... to be courageous.

And, if we were made, not an accident, but fearfully and wonderfully made, by an intelligent, benevolent being, then ... it stands to reason that we were also made for a purpose. After all, why would an intelligent, reasoning, loving and logical God create other beings without purpose? We find over and over again, by looking at the world around us, that people without purpose are driven to madness and depression, even terrible acts of violence, such as suicide and mass shootings. And what is that purpose? Why did God create us?

> God made you to be courageous and to lead the way.

Think about your reasons for becoming a parent, and it may become clear to you. You created your children, so you'd have someone to love. God created His children so He could love us as well. If we can love our own children, with all our flaws and shortcomings, then how much more magnificent is God's love for His children? For us. All of us.

God made us to be many things, but the one thing this song reveals is this. God made us to be courageous. We were fearfully and wonderfully made in God's image. Do you really believe that God is afraid; that he's a coward; that He prowls the universe in the shadows, hides from danger, going out of His way to mind His own business, selfishly doing only what is in His own best interest. If that were true, we never would have been created.

I know that I disappointed my parents from time to time. I know there were times they may have asked the question "Why did I create that boy?" My own children have disappointed me at times. But I still love them, and I will still die for them if that's what's needed to save them.

> *But God demonstrates his own love for us in this: While we were still sinners, Christ died for us.*
>
> *Romans 5:8 (NIV)*

3. We were made to lead the way.

Think about the people in the Bible that you respect, revere and admire. Is it Judas, who betrayed Christ? Is it King Herod, filled with greed? Is it Pharaoh, hardhearted and arrogant? The obvious answer is no.

We admire Joshua for his courage. We admire Paul for his steadfast resolution. We admire Moses because, despite his fear, he obeyed God and stood up to the most powerful kingdom of his time.

We were made to be courageous, because God admires courage. All these people we revere and admire were leaders, people who, despite their fear, chose to obey God rather than men. They were brave men who stood up against the evil of the world to lead the way.

Fear is a prerequisite to courage. Without fear there can be no bravery. Fear is the thing we overcome. We were made by God to be overcomers, to be leaders, to be ... courageous.

> *When you go to war against*
> *your enemies and see horses*
> *and chariots and an army*
> *greater than yours, do not be*
> *afraid of them, because the Lord*
> *your God, who brought you up*
> *out of Egypt, will be with you.*
>
> *Deuteronomy 20:1 (NIV)*

In the movie, *Courageous*, the men of God take a resolution before God and their families, promising many virtuous things. I took that pledge as well, in front of God, in front of my family, and I signed it. Now, it sits on my desk, staring at me, reminding me of who God wants me to be.

The very first line reads as follows:

> *I do solemnly resolve before*
> *God to take full responsibility*
> *for myself, my wife, and my*
> *children.*

That is huge. Full responsibility is a lot; it's all encompassing, leaving nothing good to chance. You have a duty to protect your family, and I'm not talking about just the men here ... but also you women as well. When evil comes knockin' the parents get rockin.' That's the way it has to be for the family to survive and even flourish.

And that evil can take many forms. It could be the person holding a knife against your wife's throat. It could be the pedophile who is trying to hurt your children. It could be the hormone-laden, selfish teenage boy who wants to sully your daughter's good name. Another promise in the *Courageous* pledge reads as follows:

> *I WILL love them, protect them,*
> *serve them, and teach them the*
> *Word of God as the spiritual*
> *leader of my home.*

To love .. is also to ... protect.

We naturally want to protect the ones we love. And that protection requires courage. It's one of our parental tools, and it's every bit as important as the gun I carry on my belt. The challenge with the gun, is it will not always be with you.

You are commissioned by God to protect your family whether you are armed or open-handed. Because of the myriad of laws that criss-cross our nation, you may be disarmed from time to time. But the three things you will always have is your courage, your faith in God, and your love for your spouse and children.

Courage is not passed on through your bloodline. You have to earn it with your actions.

I'm reminded of a quote from the 1991 movie, *Robin Hood: Prince of Thieves*, that inspired me as well. There was an exchange between Robin Hood (played by Kevin Costner) and Will Scarlett (played by Christian Slater) where Will asks Robin:

> *"What would you have us do, fight armored men on horseback with rocks and bare hands?"*
>
> *"If needs be. But with the one true weapon that escapes you, Will. Courage."*

Courage can always be with you. It's your birthright before God, but you must choose to accept it and exercise it.

Now, I know many of you might be thinking how naive I am right now, saying, "But Skip, you don't know the life I've lived, how hard it's been for me."

Well, that may not be true. My life has been a bit rocky as well, and I view myself as a chain breaker. When first starting out, I had very humble beginnings. My parents were poor, my father a factory worker. His own parents were of World War One and depression-era vintage. My grandfather was an almost lifelong alcoholic, and I'm sure that affected my own father. We all affect our children, for good or ill. But I recall the one thing my father said to me that molded me more than any other, "Son, the best part of you went running down your mother's leg."

That pronouncement of my father forged chains around my heart that I've struggled to break for decades now. But it was a curse that only God could break. And God did break that curse.

> I exist to protect my children, not just physically, but spiritually as well.

When I started life, I had grand and glorious dreams for myself. I was going to write the all-American novel, win the Pulitzer prize, become famous and rich. That didn't happen. However, I did work hard to break the curse for my children. Here's one thing I've learned: my true legacy, isn't in the books I write, or the radio shows I produce; it's in the way that I live my life in front of my children for all to see. A man's true legacy is in living a life for Christ, having faith in God and obeying His commands. I live my life to break the chains and free my children.

I exist to protect my children, not just physically, but also spiritually. I model, as best I can, faith and love in God. If you've had a rough past, that doesn't rule out a beautiful future, serving God and the ones you love. But the one thing you'll need to be successful in life, and the thing you'll need to pass on to your kids is courage.

No matter what happens in life, no matter how discouraged you get ... you'll need courage. Notice that the words "courage" and "discourage" are very similar but have opposite meanings.

Always remember that we were not made by God to be discouraged. We were made to be courageous.

The last line in that song by *Casting Crowns* is this:

> *"Seek Justice, Love Mercy, Walk humbly with our God."*

To do that you'll need courage, self-sacrifice and, above all, love for the ones you are sworn to protect. If you haven't yet heard the song *Courageous* by the group *Casting Crowns*, then please do so now. And if you haven't viewed the movie *Courageous* by Stephen and Alex Kendrick, then drop everything you're doing right now and get it done.

It will change you and your children ... forever.

You can purchase "Concealed Carry for Christians" on Amazon now. Available in paperback, hard cover, ebook and audiobook.

Skip Coryell lives with his wife and children in Michigan. He works full time as a professional writer, and *Sunrise Reflections* is his 19th published book. He is an avid hunter and sportsman, a Marine Corps veteran, and a graduate of Cornerstone University. You can listen to Skip as he co-hosts the syndicated military talk radio show *Frontlines of Freedom* on frontlinesoffreedom.com. You can also hear his weekly podcast *The Home Defense Show* at homedefenseshow.com.

For more details on Skip Coryell, or to contact him personally, go to his website at skipcoryell.com

Books by Skip Coryell

We Hold These Truths
Bond of Unseen Blood
Church and State
Blood in the Streets
Laughter and Tears
RKBA: Defending the Right to Keep and Bear Arms
Stalking Natalie
The God Virus
The Shadow Militia
The Saracen Tide
The Blind Man's Rage
Civilian Combat - The Concealed Carry Book
Jackpine Strong
Concealed Carry for Christians
The Covid Chronicles: Surviving the Upgrade
The Covid Chronicles: Surviving the Apocalypse
The Covid Chronicles: Surviving the Solstice
The Mad American - Judgment Day
Sunrise Reflections: Finding Hope in Hard Times
Self Defense Scenarios: Staying Alive in a Dangerous World

The God Virus
The Shadow Militia
Complete God Virus series!
The Saracen Tide
The Blind Man's Rage
Skip Coryell

This is 4 books in one! The complete 4-book God Virus apocalyptic adventure series beneath one cover. Suddenly, the lights went out, not just in one town or village, but all across the world. It was an act of cyber terrorism that plunged the world into the heart of darkness, into the 1000-year night, letting loose the demons of a billion souls, pitting dark against light, causing each person everywhere to choose sides. Not since Stephen King's "The Stand" has there been an apocalyptic thriller of such epic proportions. Read the entire 4-book series and see what happens when society's thin veneer of civility is stripped away. "The God Virus" series is gripping, seething and oozing with the best and worst humanity has to offer.

I started carrying a pistol almost 20 years ago, and I've been a member of a church safety team for about 15 years now. The church safety team is like other ministries in that we are serving the body of Christ, but there is one very distinct and important difference. It might get you killed.

I've been a Sunday school teacher, even Sunday School Superintendent. I've served on musical teams. I've been an usher. I've even helped in the children's ministry where they expected me to dance up and down to silly songs while making ridiculous hand motions. (Thank God there are no existing pictures for that one. It wasn't pretty.)

However, none of those jobs ever required me to take a bullet for the flock. As a Sunday School teacher, I was never expected to run towards gunshots while drawing my firearm. Most Sunday School teachers don't carry pepper spray; they don't practice open-handed skills to become proficient at taking a man to the ground and putting him in zip ties. They are not trained in the subtle arts of interrogation and visually identifying physical threats, like who is armed and who is not.

It's a different kind of ministry, requiring a different kind of Christian. However, all these concerns are not restricted to the church safety team, because they apply to any Christian who decides to carry a gun.

If you are considering carrying a gun or joining a church safety team, then, this book is a must-listen for you. You should not go into the job lightly, as there are many things to consider. Can you take a human life? Killing a fellow human being is not and should not be a natural and easy thing to do. It should be tough. It may take years of prayer and study and self-reflection before you decide the answer. Do you want to carry a gun? It's a nuisance, a total life change, and a bona fide pain in the butt. Carrying a gun dictates every facet of your life: how you treat others, what you wear, how you talk, and how you walk. It's not for everyone.

Are you willing to die to protect the ones you love? How about strangers? Will you die to protect someone you haven't even met yet. Are you willing to spend lots of time and money on training and equipment? Less than one percent of the concealed carry population ever go on to take training that is not required by the government. That statistic should scare you.

Buying a gun doesn't make you a gun fighter any more than buying a guitar makes you a rock star. We are called by God to excellence in everything we do. The gun is a powerful tool. The sacrifice you make could be supreme. It is a life-or-death decision. This book was written to empower and encourage Christians who decide to carry concealed. You are an elite corps of individuals. You are warriors. Welcome to the club! - Skip Coryell

If masculinity is toxic, then Jack Ruger is the cultural equivalent of a raging bull on steroids. Born and raised in the cold and frozen northern paradise of Michigan's upper peninsula, Chief of Police Jack Ruger is sworn to protect and defend the citizens of Jackpine. So when escaped killer Bobby Lee Harper descends on the town, threatening to kill him and all he holds dear, it's a formal declaration of war, and only one man will survive.

More and more people across the country are seeing the dangers in society and deciding to carry concealed to protect themselves and their families. Skip's book lays it out step by step, teaching you how to protect and defend the ones you love. Read his book and get the benefit of his 19 years of teaching experience and his lifetime of training for this important role in society. *Civilian Combat* is also a great teaching tool for other concealed carry instructors as well. It's a complete curriculum with a final test as well as important points to remember and a list of excellent resources in your journey to personal and family protection.

Skip is the creator and host of *The Home Defense Show*, a weekly 1-hour podcast about all things home, family and personal defense.

The Home Defense Show podcast is now available on iHeart, iTunes, Google Play, Spreaker and Sticher. You can also find it on my YouTube channel. This should make it easier than ever for you to listen to my sweet angelic voice coming to you from deep inside the bowels of a great big empty. Don't forget to subscribe.
For more info go to homedefenseshow.com

FRONTLINES OF FREEDOM RADIO

You can hear authors Denny Gillem and Skip Coryell on one of your local stations on the number 1 military talk show in America. *Frontlines of Freedom* is syndicated on over 180 stations, and is also available as a podcast on frontlinesoffreedom.com.

Made in the USA
Columbia, SC
16 January 2023